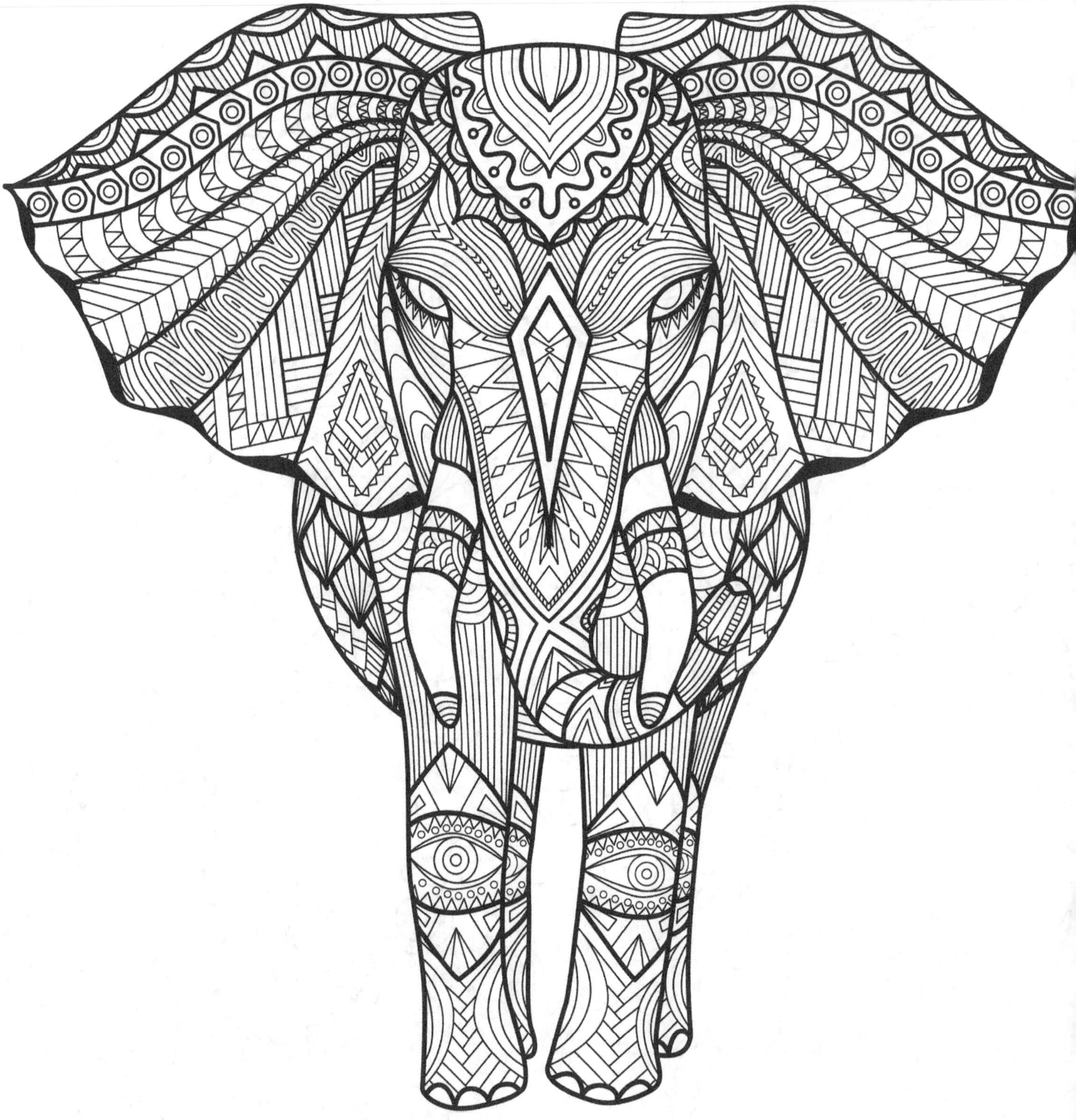

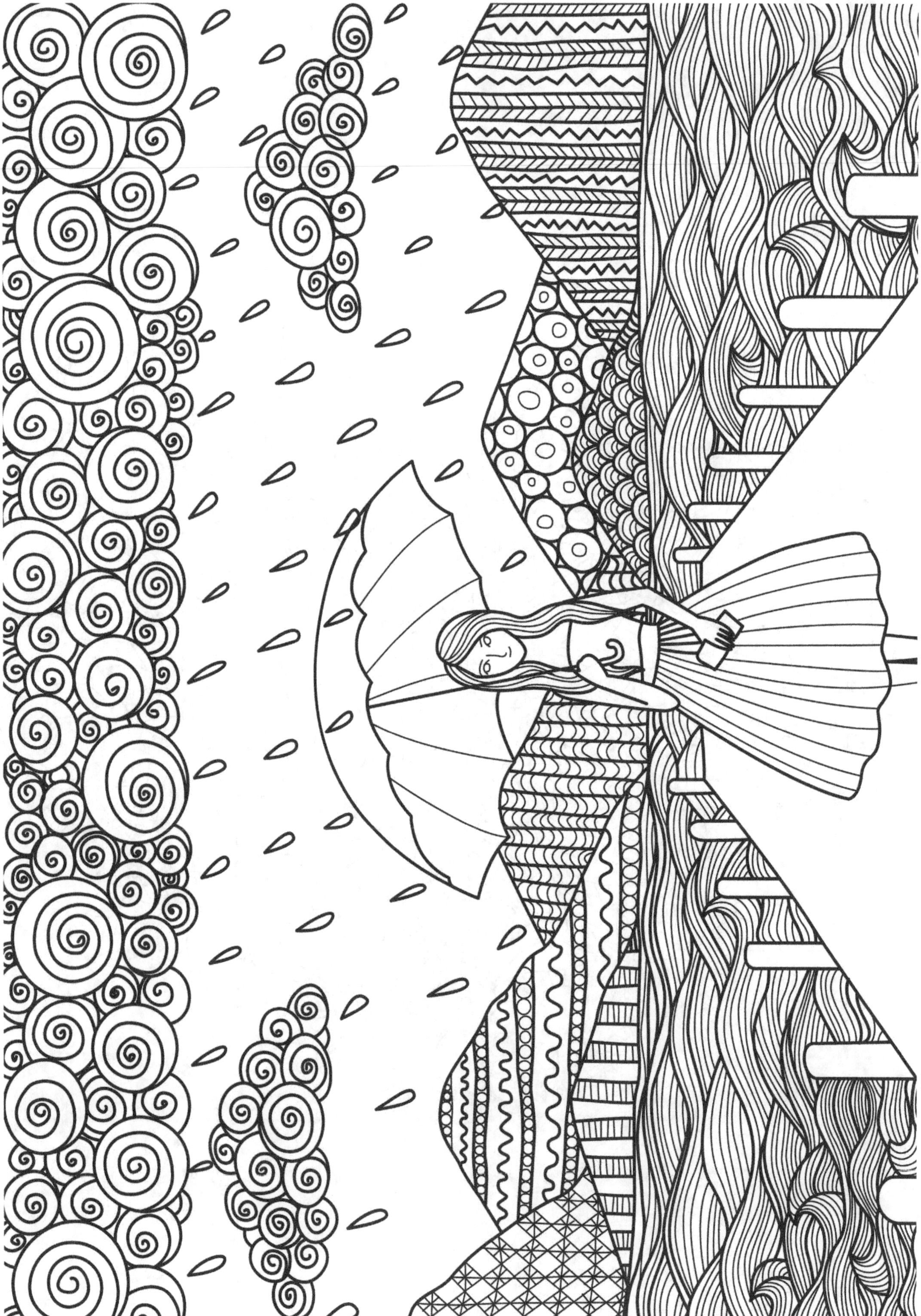

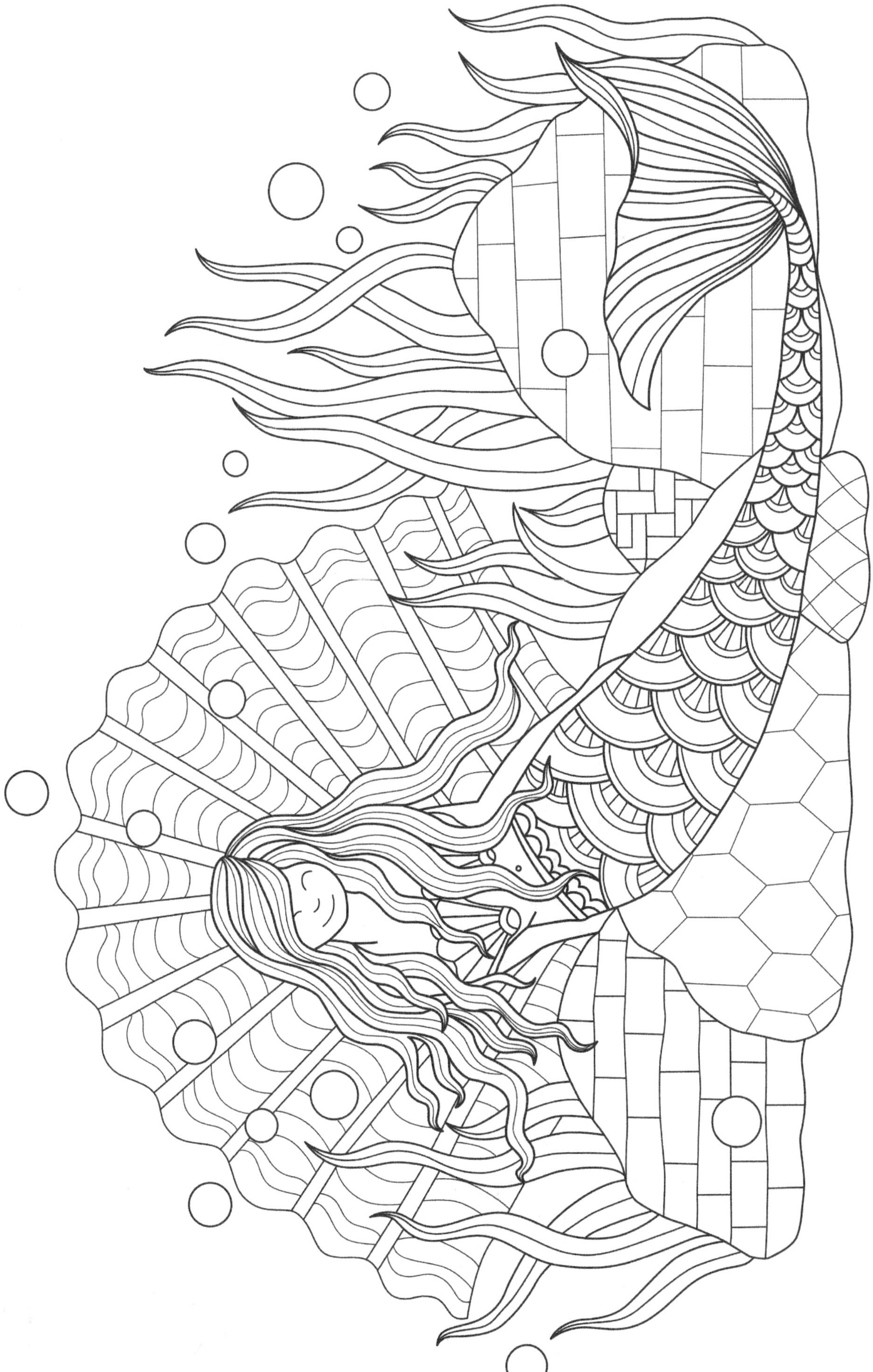

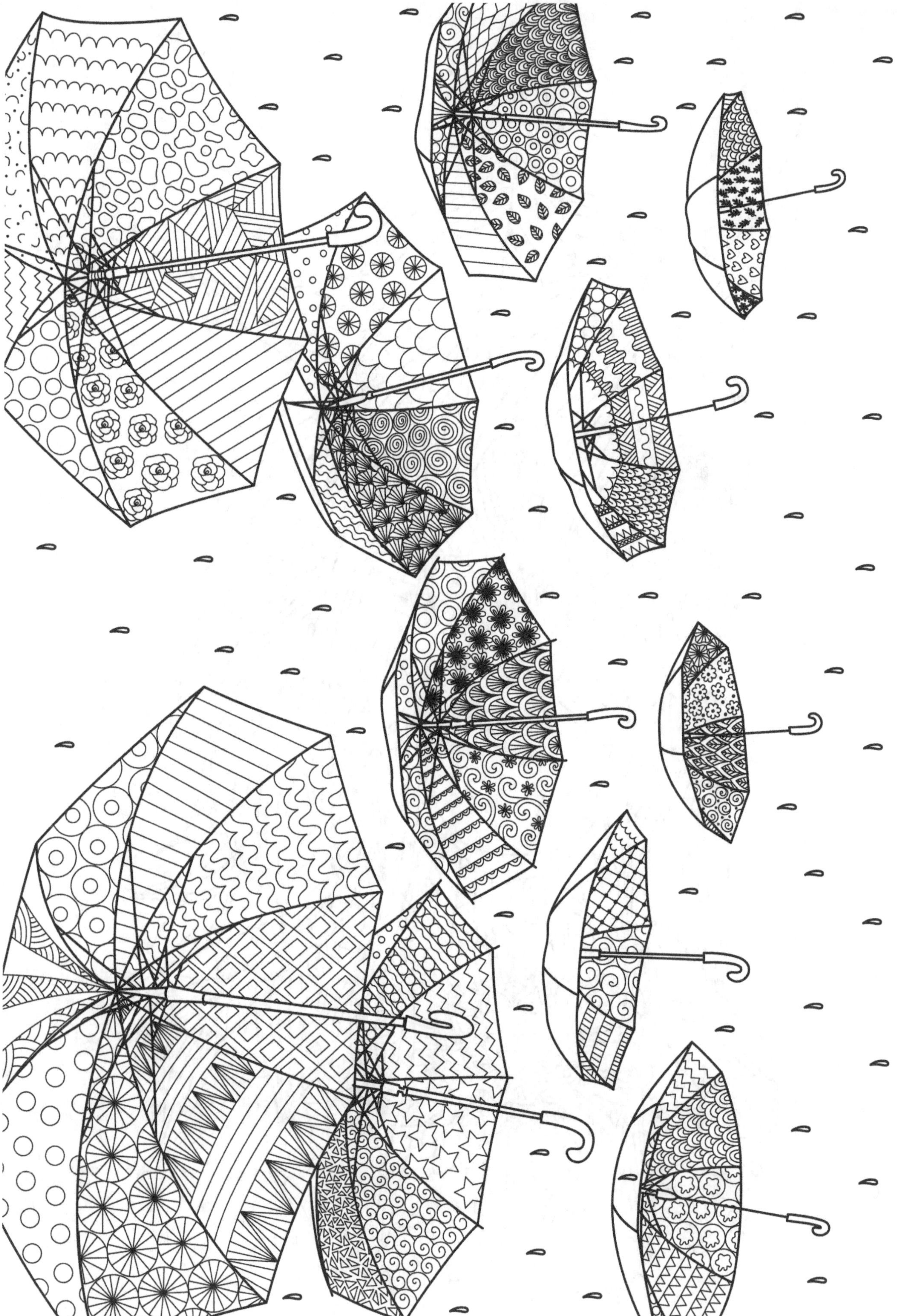

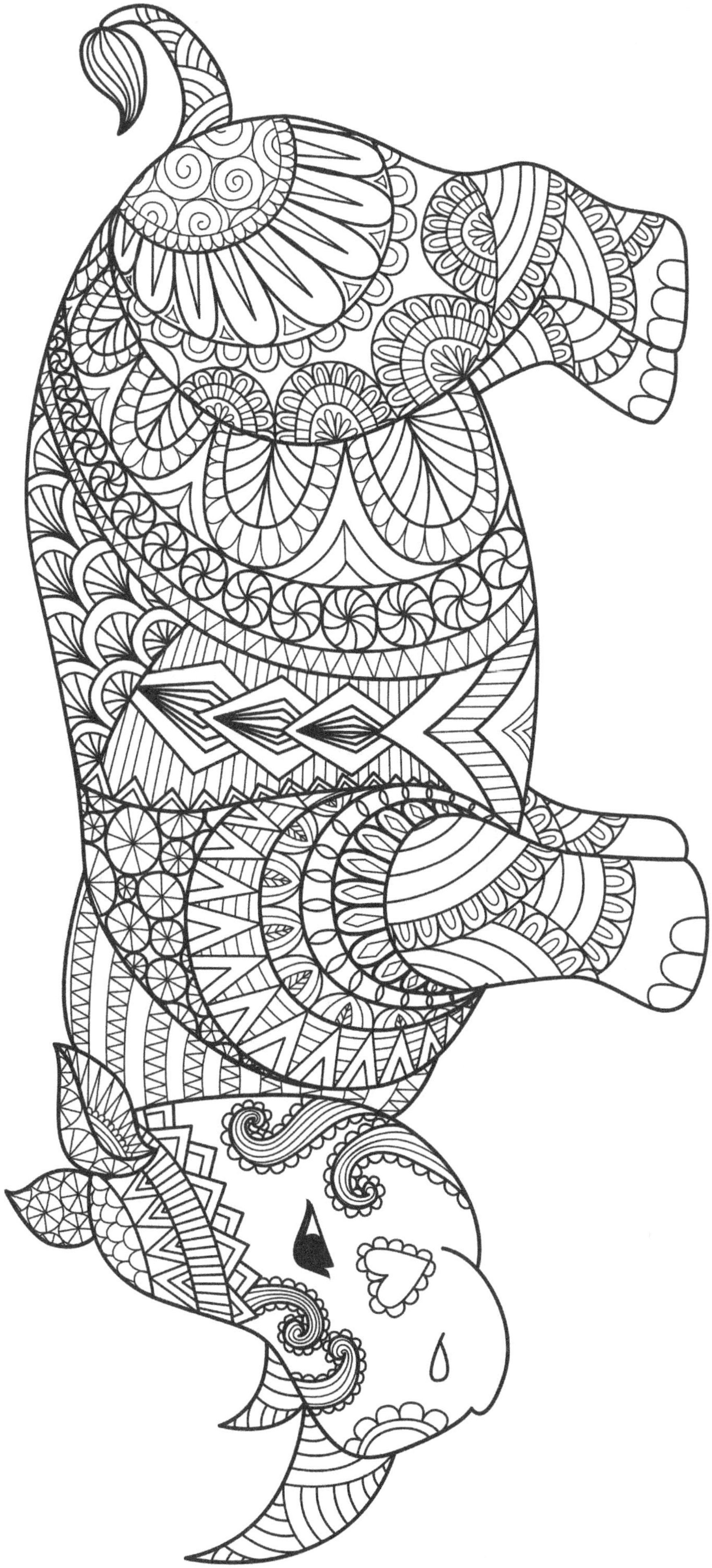

LOVE

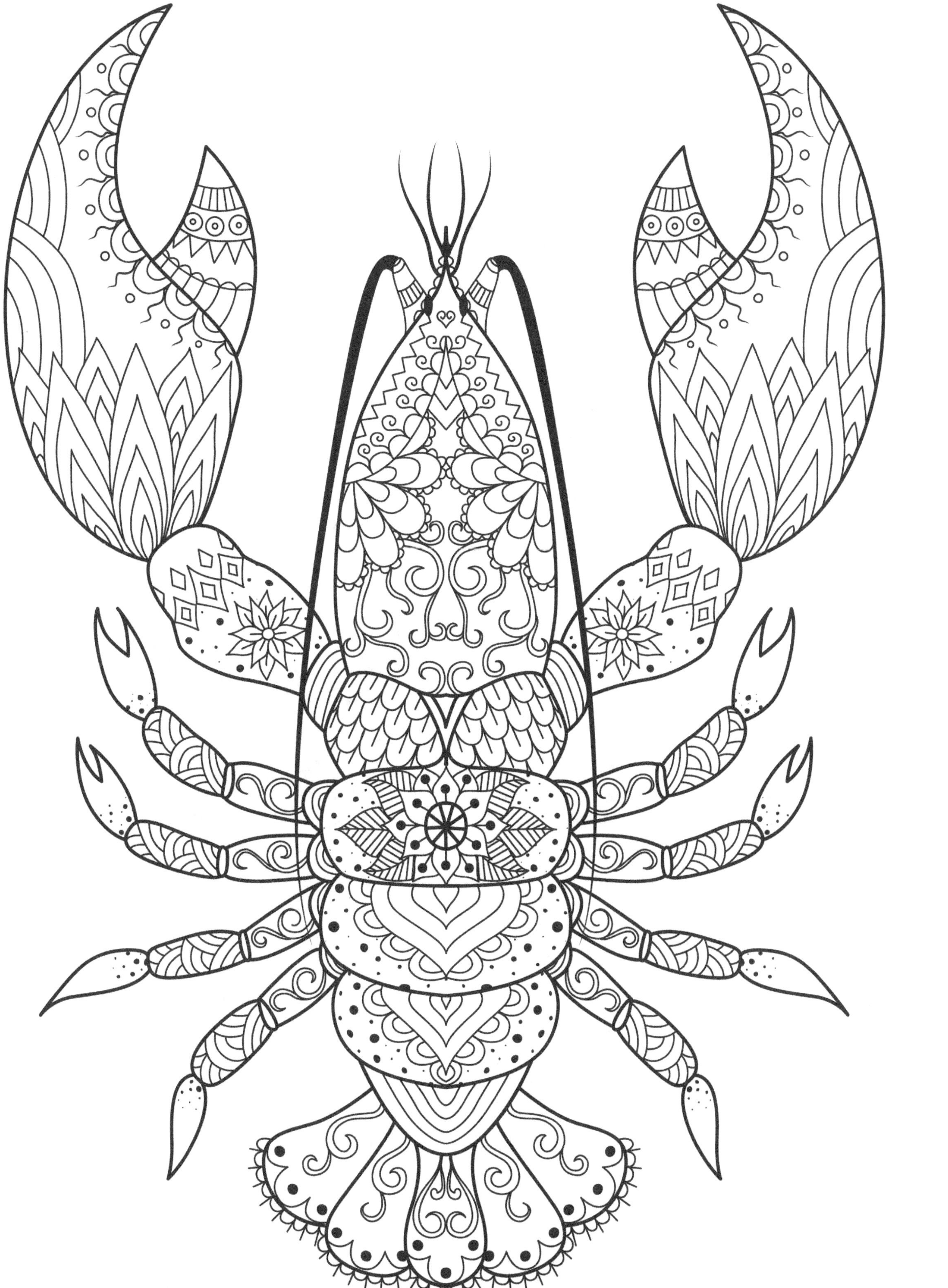

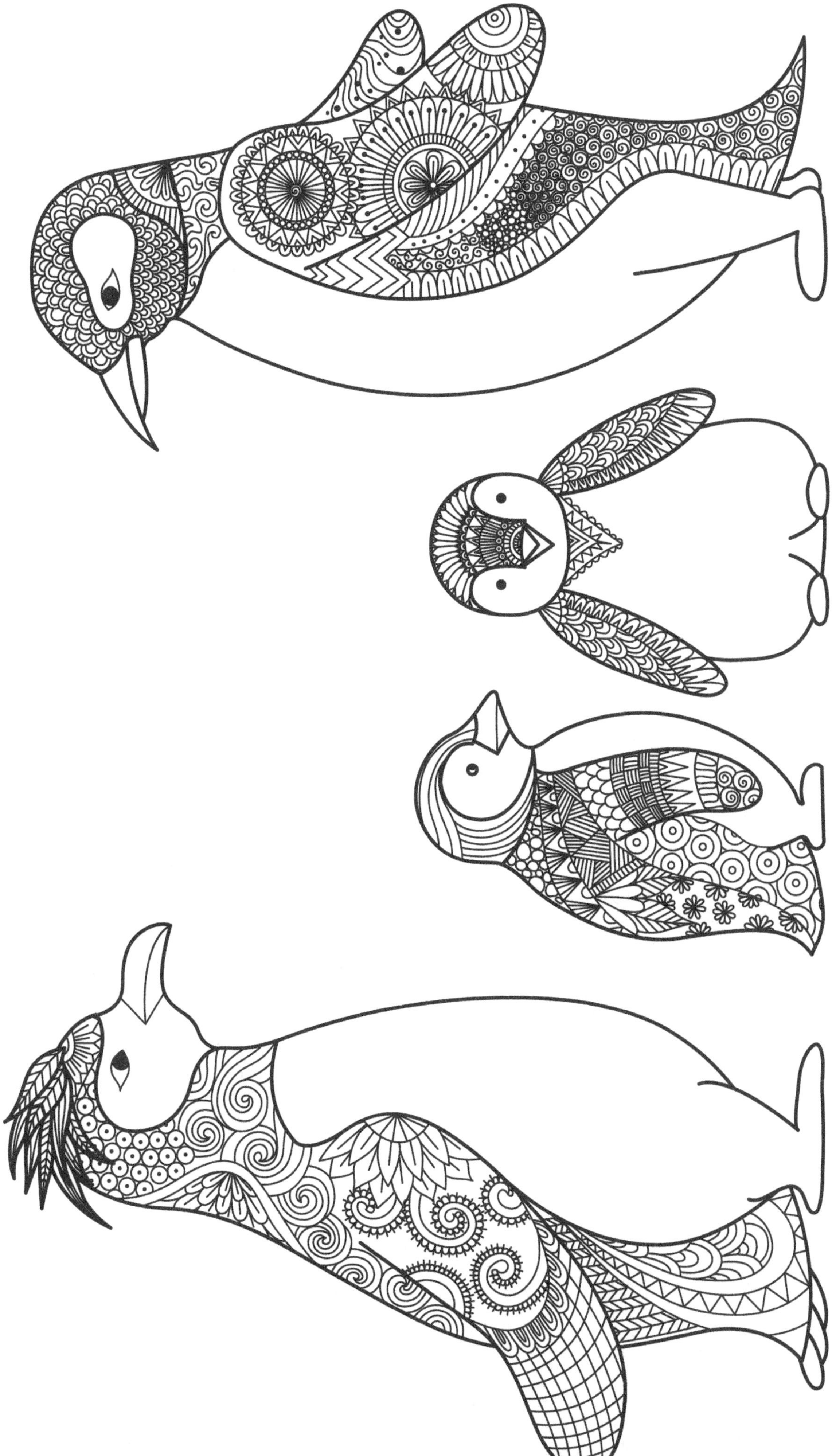

LOVE
you

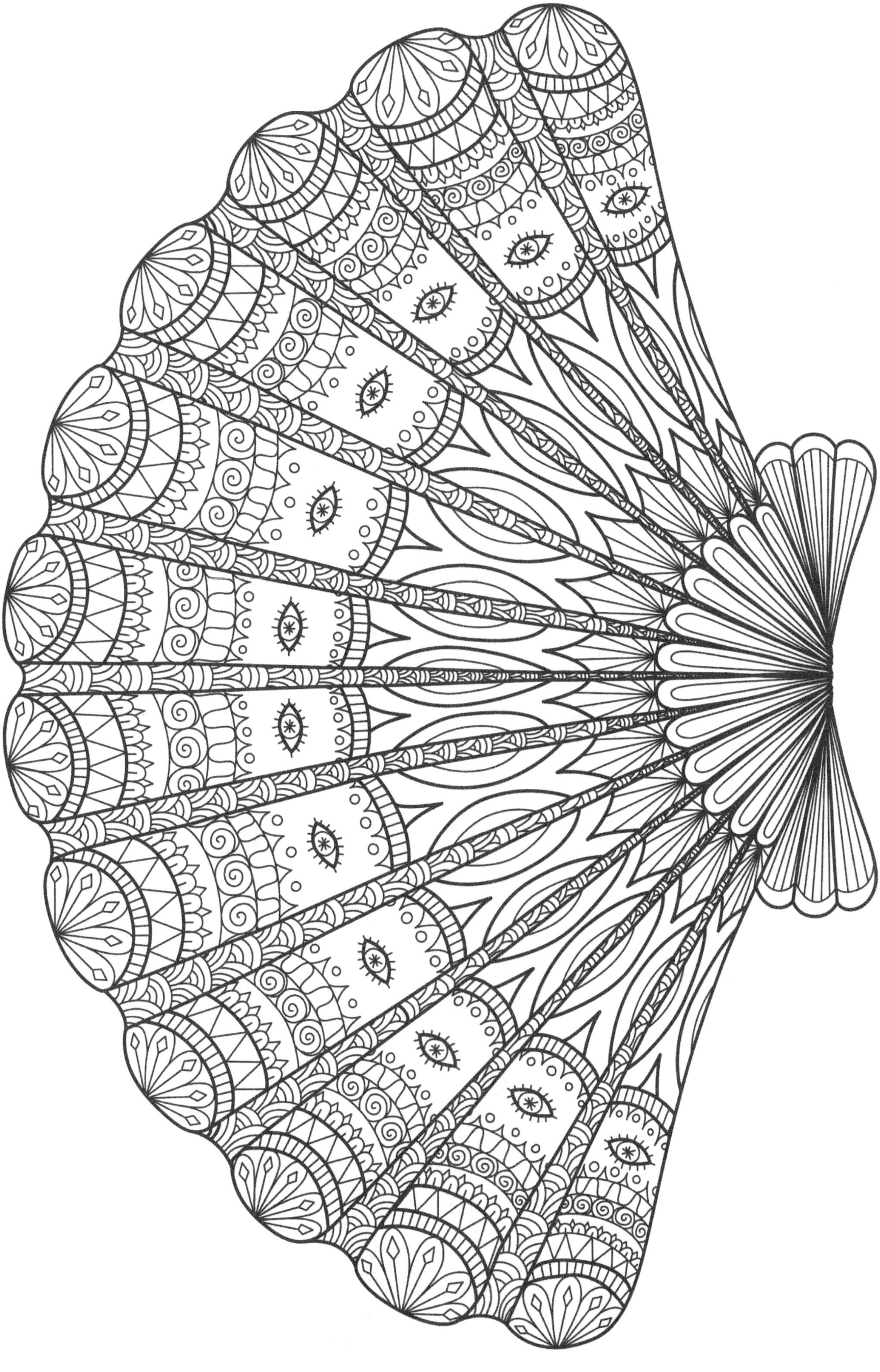

Mandala

Love

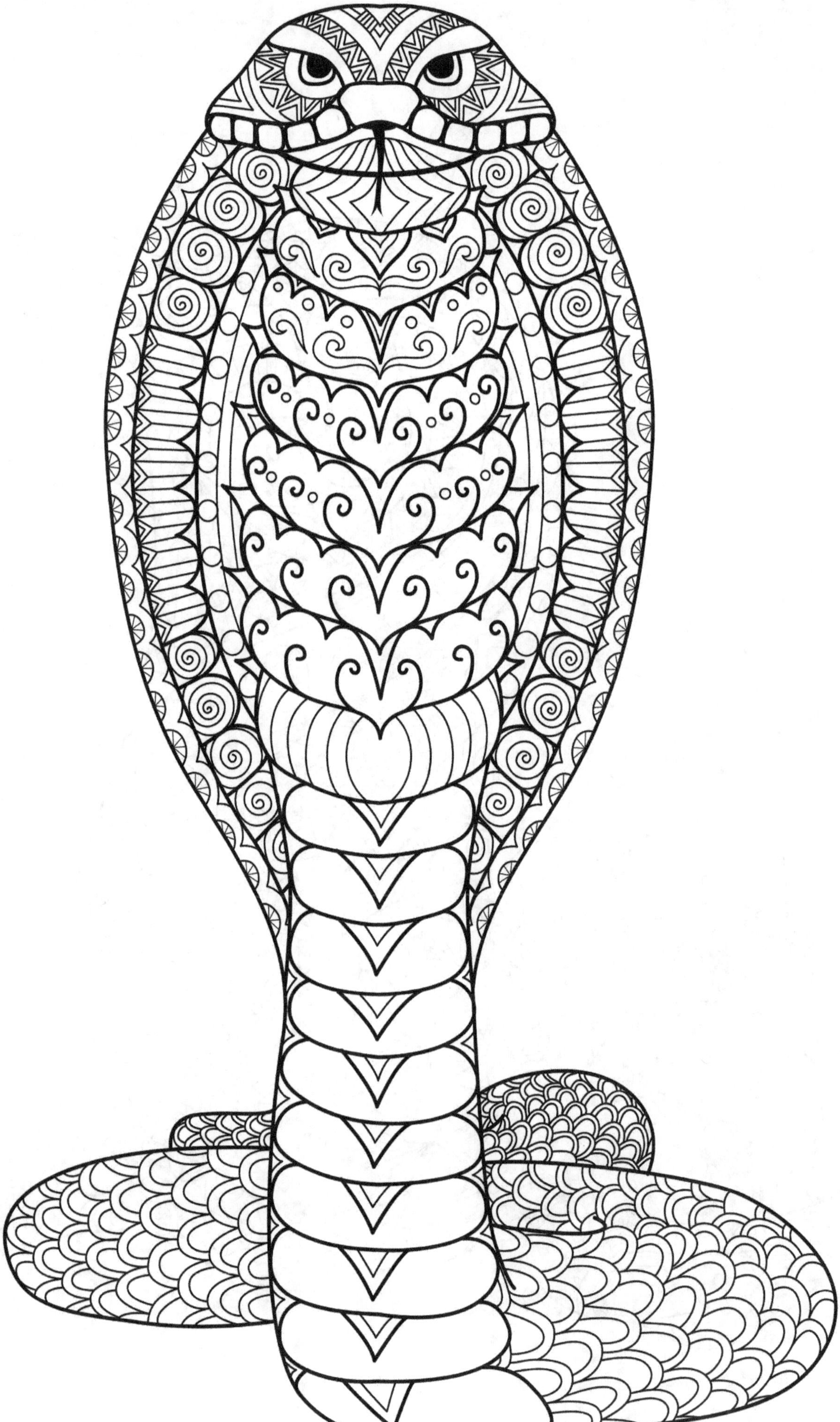

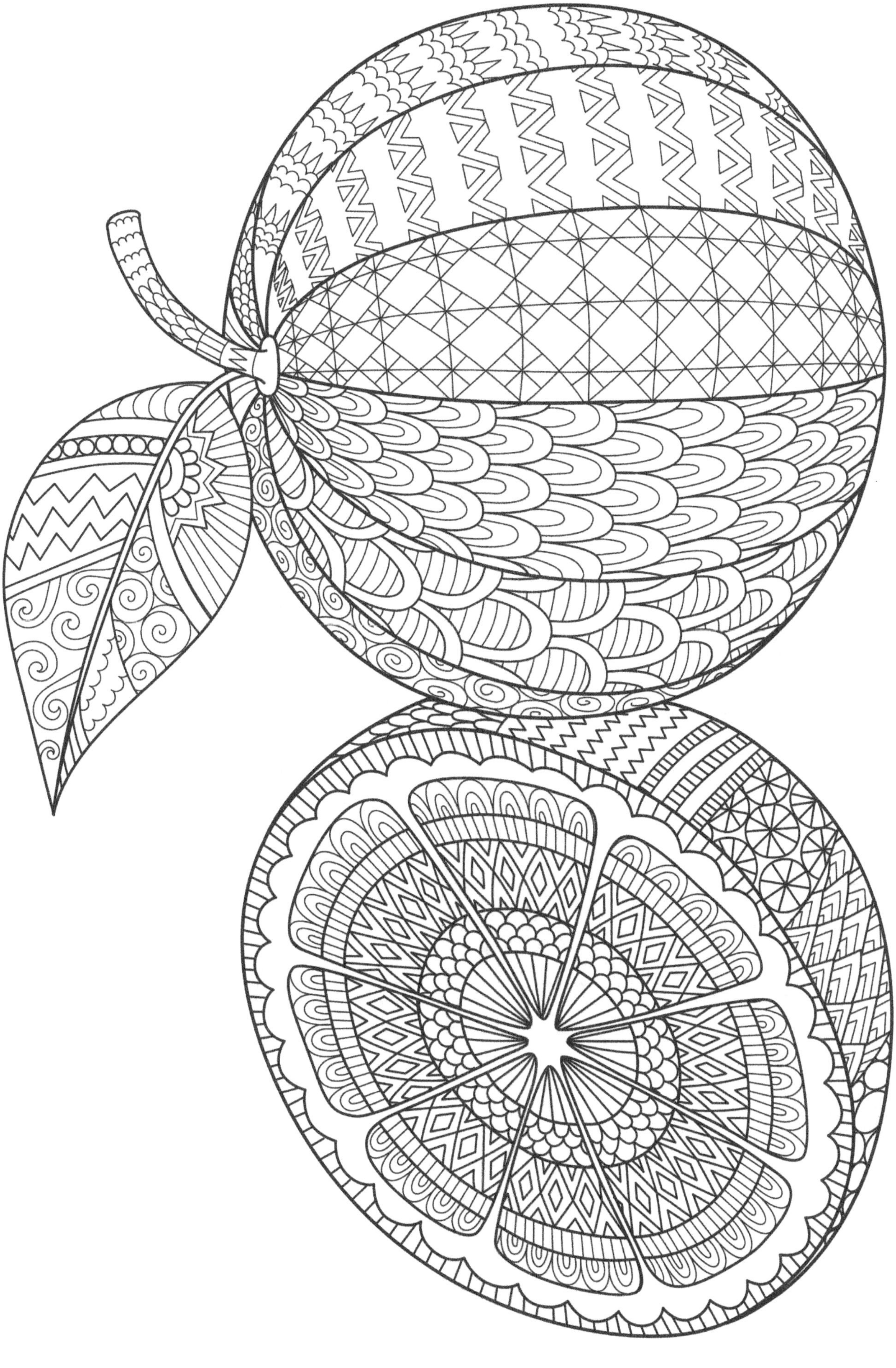

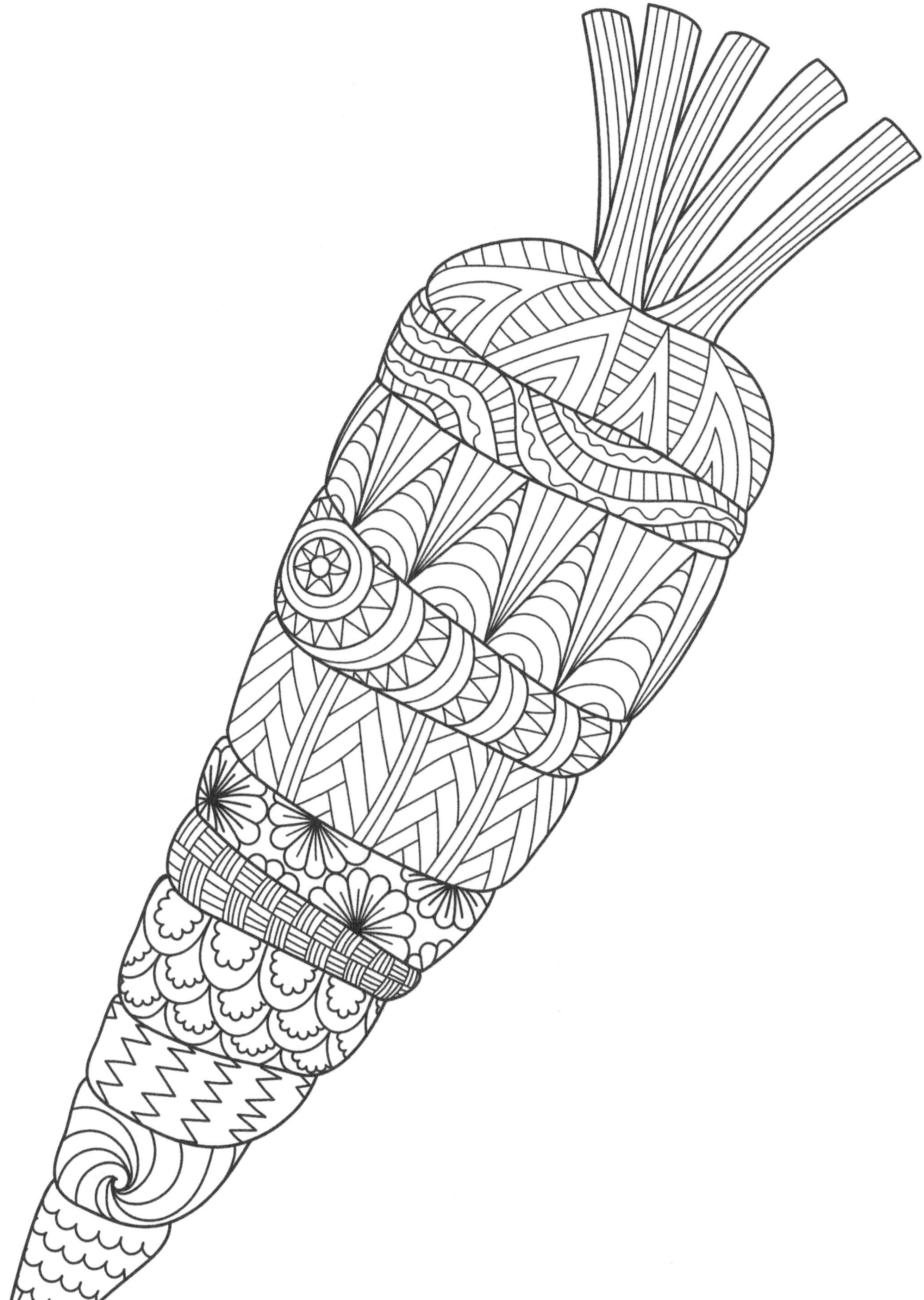

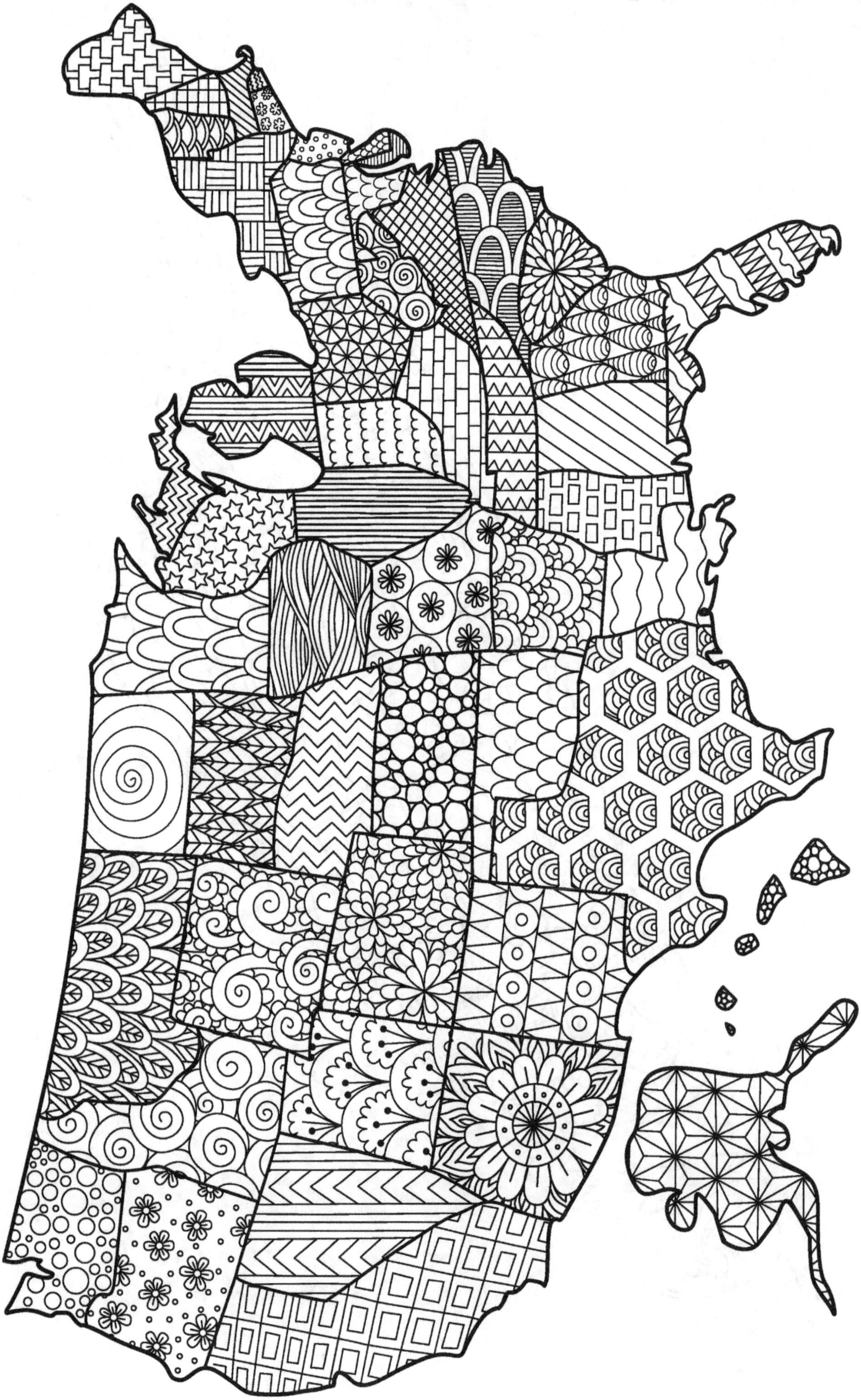

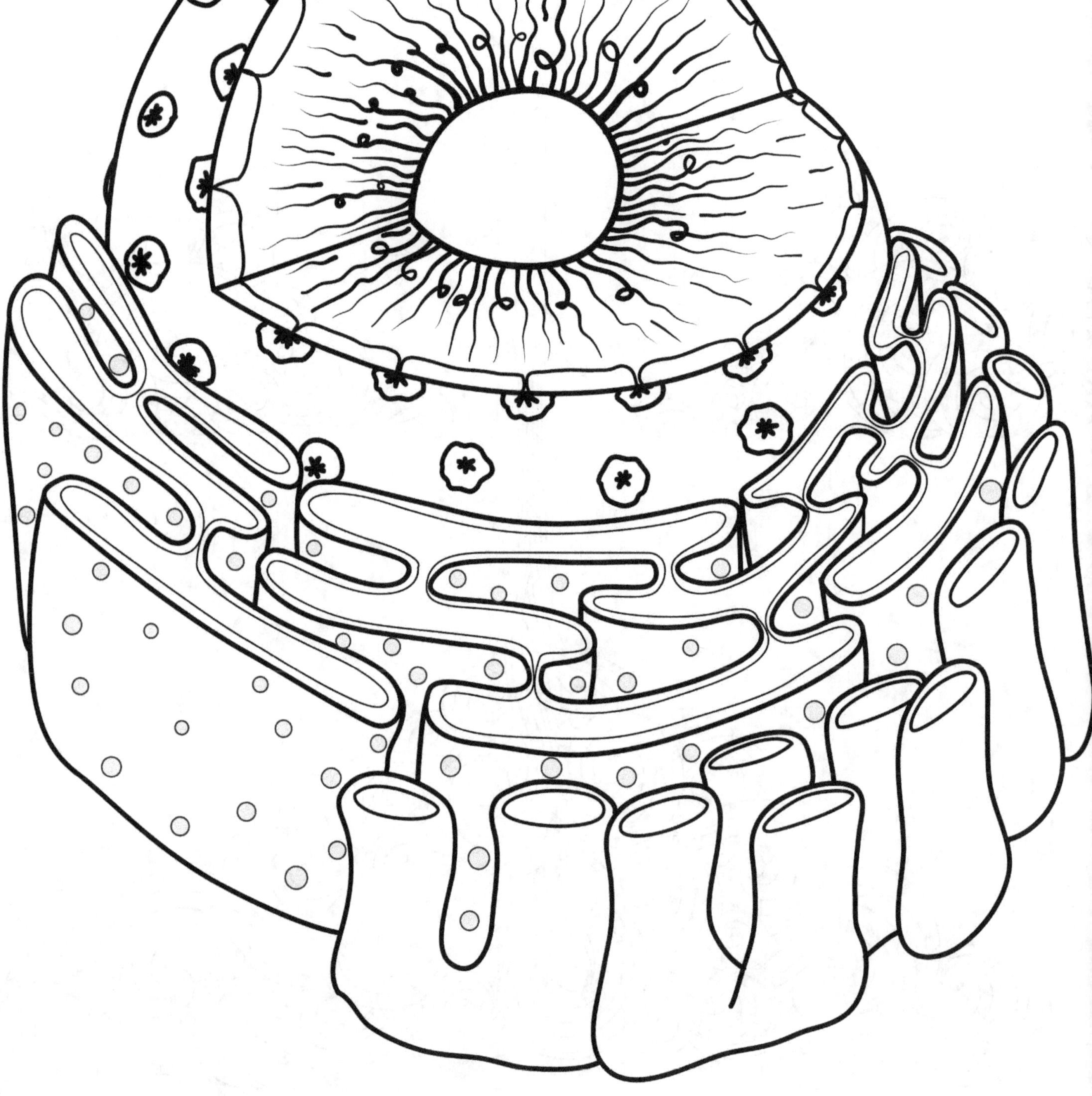

love

TAURUS

GEMINI

♌

LEO

Merry Christmas

www.ingramcontent.com/pod-product-compliance
Lightning Source LLC
Chambersburg PA
CBHW081306250726
48662CB00008B/2424
* 9 7 8 1 6 7 5 7 6 9 7 5 1 *